Larry Burkett's

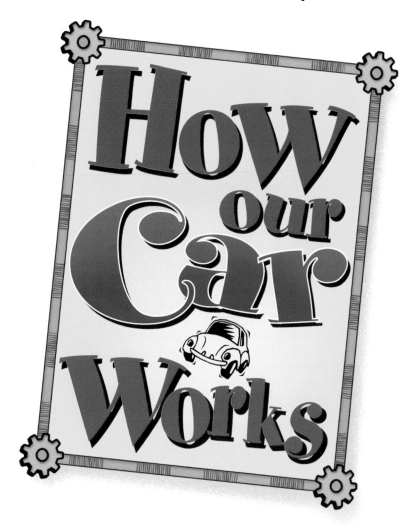

How our Car Works

written by Ed Strauss

illustrated by Ed Letwenko

Larry Burkett's
Stewardship
for the Family
www.4kids.org
Time Talents & Treasures

Faith Parenting Guide
Ages 7 and up
Stewardship

Faith KiDs
Equipping Kids for Life
faithkids.com

A Faith Building Guide
can be found on page 32.

Faith Kids® is an imprint of Cook Communications Ministries,
Colorado Springs, Colorado 80918
Cook Communications, Paris, Ontario
Kingsway Communications, Eastbourne, England

HOW OUR CAR WORKS ©2002 by Burkett & Kids, LLC

First printing, 2002
Printed in Singapore.
1 2 3 4 5 6 7 8 9 10 Printing/Year 06 05 04 03 02

Larry Burkett's Stewardship for the Family
Executive Producer: Allen Burkett

Lightwave Publishing
Concept Direction: Rick Osborne

Cook Communications Ministries
Senior Editor: Heather Gemmen
Designer: Keith Sherrer, iDesignEtc.

Library of Congress Cataloging-in-Publication Data

Burkett, Larry.
    How our car works / Larry Burkett with Ed Strauss.
        p. cm.
    Summary: Rhyming text and illustrations detail various facts about
cars and car maintenance including purchasing a car, brake systems,
steering, safety, and driving laws, all from a Christian perspective.
    ISBN 0-7814-3792-X
    1. Automobiles--Juvenile literature. 2. Automobile
driving--Juvenile literature. 3. Children--Religious life--Juvenile
literature. 4. Christian life--Juvenile literature. [1. Automobiles.
2. Christian life.]   I. Strauss, Ed, 1953-   . II. Title.

TL147 .B847 2002
629.222--dc21
                            2001005183

Mick Kanik

WELCOME TO MY SHOP! Mick Kanik's the name!

I love car mechanics, fixing cars is my game.

If you're headed to school, the movies, or mall,

You'll ride in "Mom's Taxi" if you get there at all.

So care for your taxi—yes, make your car last—

If you want to go places and you want to go fast. ☼

MY FULLY RESTORED 1969 BABY:
I worked on this in my spare time all last year.

Financial Systems

THE JUDDS ARE OUT SHOPPING for a good second car.

(When Dad drives to work, Mom and kids can't go far.)

Since new cars cost plenty and used ones work well,

The Judds came to Burton's to see what they sell.

They took me along to inspect their top choices,

To listen for whining and bumpy-grind noises.

Cars cost bucks to buy, to care for and run,

So it's best to be careful and choose the right one.

The Judds saved their money; they built up a stash.

When it comes time to pay, they will pay with cold cash.

Each family is different with needs of their own,

But saving, then spending, costs less than a loan. ✿

THE LAW SAYS you must buy automobile insurance to pay expenses in case you have an accident. (Your parents keep these papers in the glove compartment of the car.)

THE AVERAGE COST of a new car is $20,000; the average cost of a good second-hand car is $10,000.

I AM CHECKING what shape the engine is in. Good so far.... I haven't found any oil leaks.

IF YOU TAKE OUT a bank loan to buy your car, you will have to pay the bank hundreds or thousands of dollars in interest payments.

THIS MAN in the background is leasing a car instead of buying it. It costs more, but his business needs him to always drive a new car.

TOM IS ASKING the salesman if the car has been in an accident. It looks like the passenger's front door has been repaired, then repainted.

5

Engine Systems

WHAT MAKES TIRES TURN on the big McDuff van?

Not mice on conveyer belts turning a fan.

"Internal combustion" sends them down the road

To Zingo's Pet Store to buy flies for Bill's toad.

Gas sprays in the chamber from a tank in the back.

It mixes with air and the spark plugs go "Zzzak!"

A spark enters the gas well and causes a blast,

And all the explosions make the pistons pump fast.

This moves the crankshaft, which turns the transmission,

Which turns the drive shaft and sets wheels in motion.

These explosions and turnings cause the van to run fast—

If Scott can remember to fill it with gas. ☀

"INTERNAL" means "inside" and "combustion" means "explosion," so an internal combustion engine is an engine with explosions inside it.

HERE WE SEE fuel (pumped from the gas tank in back) coming through fuel lines and being sprayed into the combustion chamber.

IN AUTOS with a fuel injection system, computers control the way gas is sprayed into the combustion chamber where it mixes with air.

GENERALLY, car motors have 4 to 6 pistons. This engine has 8 pistons. When an explosion in the combustion chamber pushes a piston back, it moves in a circular motion called "torque," which turns the crankshaft around.

TODAY THERE ARE "hybrid" cars that have both electric motors and internal combustion engines. The car's computer will switch from one system to the other, depending on what kind of driving you're doing.

Control Systems

JACK HO NEEDS CONTROL when he steps on the gas,
Or he'd be off the highway and right in the grass.
He'd be in the cornfields with cows on his hood
If he didn't grip the wheel as tight as he should.

His 4x4 is a "standard" that lets him move quick.
He steps on the clutch and shifts gears with the stick.
First gear gives him power when he's going slow;
Fourth gear gives him speed when he's raring to go.

The kind of transmission—let me be quite emphatic—
That shifts by itself is called "automatic."
Be careful in both cars of buttons or gears,
Or you'll land in a ditch with mud in your ears.

SEE THE HORN on the steering wheel? Jack is courteous and only honks his horn when he needs to warn other vehicles.

WITH A STANDARD, you move the gear stick to "shift" your engine into first, second, third, fourth, fifth gear, or reverse. The position in the center is neutral.

AUTOMATIC: You still have to shift a few gears in an automatic—out of park into drive or into reverse—but it's a lot less work.

CRUISE CONTROL: When Jack is on a straight highway, he presses these buttons to switch to "cruise." Then he takes his foot off the gas and "cruises" at a steady speed.

IN AUTOS with "power steering," just a light touch on the steering wheel turns the vehicle.

THE DRIVE SHAFT connects the transmission to the axles, which turn the tires.

9

Light & Electrical Systems

New trucks these days don't go for simplicity;
The Navidads' pickup has loads of electricity!
One little button moves a mirror around.
Another one makes the windows go down.

One flick and the headlights will light up the night.
Another switch makes the brake light flash right.
Martina needs light to look for the map.
To turn on the bulb is really a snap.

Up front the control panel has started to glow;
It's the gas pump symbol and means gas is low.
This is not a good sign nor a great situation:
They're still eighty miles from the next service station. ✸

IN NEW VEHICLES like the Navidads', when their gas or windshield wiper fluid is low, a door is ajar, or they need oil, a symbol lights up on the control panel.

MIGUEL SIGNALS with his lights before he turns left or right. This lets other drivers know which way he's turning, and prevents accidents.

MIGUEL SOMETIMES needs his headlights on high beam to see on a really dark road, but when a car is driving his way, he dims his lights to low beam to avoid blinding the driver.

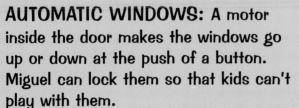

AUTOMATIC WINDOWS: A motor inside the door makes the windows go up or down at the push of a button. Miguel can lock them so that kids can't play with them.

WHEN A CAR IS RUNNING, it gets most of the electricity it needs from the alternator. The alternator also charges the battery. The battery stores electricity and supplies it to start the vehicle and run electrical systems when the engine is off.

BRAKE LIGHTS: If Miguel sees the brake lights go on in the car ahead of them, he knows that car is slowing down or stopping. He slows down to avoid ramming into them.

Tire, Brake, & Suspension Systems

Shock absorbers and tires will soften the bumps
When the Judds' van runs over potholes and humps.
The brakes must work well for all of their sakes—
They all want to stop when Mom steps on the brakes.

Good tread on the tires is important for grip;
Bald tires will make for a very bad trip.
If you're sledding down hills, sure, sliding is fun,
But sliding's not good out on Interstate One. ✿

WHEN LAURA STEPPED ON THE BRAKES, brake fluid went down the brake line and pushed the brake pads out; this made them grip the metal disc on the inside of the wheel and slow down the tires.

TIRES NEED GOOD TREAD (zig-zag grooves in the rubber) to grip the road firmly. Smooth (bald) tires slip and skid; plus, they've worn so thin they might pop.

THE JUDDS NEED A SPARE if one of their tires goes flat. This is bolted to the underside of their van. (In some vehicles the spare is under the floorboards of the trunk or attached to the back of the vehicle.)

DIFFERENT TIRES are made for different needs. "All weather" tires are good year round. Winter tires have deeper treads for driving in snow and ice; sometimes drivers even need to put chains on their tires.

HERE YOU SEE me putting new brake pads on the Judds' vehicle just before they went on this trip. That's why Laura was able to quickly stop.

A CAR'S SUSPENSION SYSTEM uses springs, shock absorbers, and hydraulics to make the ride smoother. (It keeps the axle "suspended" from the frame.)

13

Fluid Systems

When Mary McDuff pulls into the station,
The kids get big slushies to stop dehydration.
As Josh starts to race to the restroom nearby,
Scott says he should give their engine an eye.

The radiator needs water, which is noticed by Scott.
Peter checks if they've got enough oil or not.
Ann takes the gas nozzle and fills their tank full.
I check if the brake fluid line has a hole. ✿

AT THE SWITCH OF A BUTTON, windshield washer fluid is squirted up across the windshield to cut through the grease.

PETER LIFTS UP the metal "dip stick" to see how much oil is in the van. Oil lubricates ("greases") the moving parts of the engine to keep them from burning up when they rub against other parts.

GAS

WATER AND RADIATOR COOLANT fill the van's radiator. From there, they are "radiated" (circulated) around the engine to help keep the hot engine cool.

MARY SAID the brakes felt "spongy" when she stepped on them; this made me suspect there was a hole in the brake fluid line and that the fluid was leaking out.

THE GAS GAUGE (on the dashboard) lets the McDuffs know how full their gas tank is. The gauge sends an electrical signal to the spring-loaded float on the surface of the gas. When the signal comes back, it tells where the float is; an arrow on the gauge indicates the level of the gas. Here we're looking at the nozzle of the fuel pump pumping gas into van's gas tank.

TRANSMISSION FLUID lubricates the transmission and helps the gears to shift.

15

Safety Systems

What keeps Susan safe when Mom slams on the brakes
To stop them from hitting the possums and snakes?
Sue wears her seat belt and is properly seated
And knows the air bag will pop out if it's needed.

When you drive, obey rules; when you ride, behave right;
It bothers the driver if you throw things or fight.
Wrestling, throwing, yelling, and striving
Are just not allowed while Jennie is driving. ⚙

SEAT BELTS should only be unsnapped when the car has come to a full stop. Lisa will unsnap hers by hitting the release button.

AIR BAGS can save adults' lives, but they inflate (fill with air) with too much force for young kids. This is one reason kids shouldn't sit in the front seats.

CHILDREN MUST SIT in a child seat if they're not heavy or tall enough to sit on the seat by themselves.

THE BODIES OF CARS are made so that if they hit or if they are hit by something hard, they will crumple up and absorb the force of the impact. This protects passengers.

THE METAL TONGUE of Kennie's seat belt should snap firmly into place. Also, the strap itself should fit around his body snugly.

Security Systems

To keep his car safe when he's not around it
Miguel could train tigers to guard and surround it.
But who would do that? Hey, who has the time?
There are easier ways to stop auto crime.

A push of a button will lock up the door.
To set an alarm is a very small chore.
If a thief tries to break in while the owner is gone,
The alarm will wail on and wail on and wail on.

One more thing that he does to stop thieves that steal
Is to clamp a lock on his truck's steering wheel.
Miguel isn't careless. His truck is secure,
Though Pedro still wants the tigers (for sure!).

ON SOME VEHICLES, you need to lock the doors one at a time, pressing the buttons down by hand. Other cars allow you lock all doors at once with one press of a button.

A CAR STARTS by putting a key into the ignition and turning it. Never make it easy for thieves by leaving your keys in the car.

THE NAVIDADS never leave valuables lying in their car where thieves can see them. Also, they always park in a safe, well-lighted area.

NOT ALL CARS have all these security devices, but do what you can—especially remembering to lock up—to help keep your family's vehicle safe.

19

Maintenance Systems

Tom takes care of things—he maintains his car:

He checks out his engine before he goes far.

If the engine starts sounding like a mad ostrich squawk,

His kids might prefer just to get out and walk.

He makes sure there is water in the car's radiator

And the treads of his tire look like the back of a 'gator.

After three thousand miles I change the Judds' oil;

I do a full tune up, though it takes time and toil. ⚙

SPARK PLUGS should be replaced every 20,000 miles or so. If they're not working properly, they won't give good sparks, and Tom's engine won't work well.

TOM'S NEW (ACTUALLY USED) CAR has a maintenance book. This book has a tune-up schedule in it that tells him what parts of his car he should have checked up, and how often.

IT'S A GOOD THING Tom checked the water level in the battery. It had a leak, and if he hadn't caught it, his car wouldn't have started and his battery would have been ruined.

I'M CHANGING TOM'S OIL for him. I drain off the old oil into a pan (which I will dispose of in the right place), and will put in new oil.

TOM'S TIRES should contain 35 PSI (pounds per square inch) of air, but this one has only 20. It might have a small nail in it, causing a slow leak.

FILTERS

FAN BELTS

PREVENTATIVE MAINTENANCE: A small engine problem can be fixed fairly cheaply if it's caught early on. But let the malfunction go for too long, and it could cause a major, expensive repair.

Cleanup Systems

The big McDuff van had trash on its floor:

Crackers and fast food, pop cans and much more.

Kids cannot drive until they are grown,

But they can clean a van—and they don't need to moan.

Bill used the hose; Ruth scrubbed with a rag;

Ben carried off the trash in a bag;

Pete waxed the sides, then buffed till they shone;

Ann dusted the dashboard till the dust was all gone;

The rugs were all vacuumed by Sally and Bob.

Then Mom told them all, "You've done a great job!" ☼

SALLY AND HER FRIEND BOB are using small vacuum cleaner attachments to get dirt and crumbs off the floor. They took out the rugs to clean them and to vacuum beneath them.

SPRAY CLEANERS cut the grease and let you wipe windows and mirrors clean. Paper towels work better than cloth ones.

I'M PUTTING A NEW WIPER on the windshield. The rubber on the old wiper was worn down and wasn't wiping away the rain very well anymore.

IT HELPS to have a bag or box in your vehicle that you can put garbage into so that trash doesn't end up all over the floor.

WAXING AND BUFFING not only make a vehicle look nice and clean, but the wax protects it from the sun and the rain.

CAR WAX

Convenience Systems

It's great to be here in God's wild Creation,
Enjoying the comforts of civilization.
(Phones are now built right into some cars.
Mini-vans sometimes have small VCRs.)

While the stereo plays "Worship Fiesta,"
Susan reclines for a little siesta.
She sips lemonade (which had been chilling)
From a cup in a drink tray that keeps it from spilling.

Conditioning keeps them cool in a blaze;
The heater will warm them on polar cold days.
Their truck's "fully loaded," so leisures abound!
　　　They lack just a robot to drive them around. ✿

THE AIR CONDITIONING SYSTEM works great on hot days. It draws in air from outside, cools it, then sends it into the Hos' vehicle.

24

SOME NEW VEHICLES even have on-board computers that show maps, tell you where you're going, which street to turn on, and more.

RADIO, STEREO, AND SOUND SYSTEMS! This is the life! Susan can listen to her favorite CD even when they're driving over Rattlesnake Pass.

LISA PRESSES A LEVER to make her seat lean back, lifts a handle to move her entire seat forward or backward, and adjusts a headrest for maximum comfort.

Road Laws

As the Navidads drive, they see many signs.
They follow them closely to avoid all the fines.
Some give directions—the kids try to read them.
Some warn of danger—Miguel's sure to heed them. ✺

SPEED LIMIT SIGNS are there for your own safety. If you speed
(drive faster than the limit) you can't make sharp turns as easily.
It also takes longer to stop. Drivers need to be aware of the speed
limit in town because often it is not posted.

WHEN YOU'RE DRIVING past a construction site, you must
obey the flag person if they tell you to stop. It's the law.

WHEN THE DIVIDING LINE in a highway is solid, Miguel doesn't pass another car. It's dangerous. He only passes when the dividing line is broken.

DRIVER'S LICENSE:
It is illegal to drive a vehicle if you don't have a driver's license. You must carry it with you whenever you drive.

LOOK AT ALL THE SIGNS in the picture.
Do you know what each of these signs means?

27

Different Vehicles

There are so many models of autos these days.

There's a truck for each need and a car for each taste.

Pickups work best if you're hauling Rex fossils.

Big vans have the space if your family's colossal.

Some folks like sporty, fast cruising machines,

But they pick 4x4s for terrain that is mean.

Whatever you choose, talk it out with the Lord;

Pick out the car you can truly afford. ✿

IF YOUR PARENTS have a few kids, chances are good that your family owns a van. They're roomy and have the space for several children.

SPORTS CARS are fast and sleek. They often don't have room for more than two passengers, but they have powerful engines.

IF YOU WANT to drive in rugged terrain, through the mud, and in places where there are no roads, a 4x4 is your best bet.

A LUXURY CAR is an impressive, classy vehicle like a Mercedes or a Rolls Royce. They cost more to buy, but are very well made and last a long time.

A PICKUP TRUCK is great if you don't have a large family and often need to haul dirty things in the back. You can buy pickups with extended cabs to carry extra passengers.

HERE'S AN SUV (Sports Utility Vehicle). They're almost as roomy as a van, but look a little less "tame," and are often used for driving off the main roads.

Being Thankful

If you ever ride to the beach or the zoo,
Taking care of Mom's Taxi is a job for you, too.
Whether you ride in a Jag or jalopy,
Don't be laid-back or lazy or sloppy.

Do what you can to keep your car clean,
To shine it so much that no spots can be seen.
At home or at church or wherever you are,
Be thankful to God for your zooming car.

**Faith
Parenting
Guide**

**Ages
7 and up**

Stewardship

How Our Car Works

Life Issue: I want my children to learn why they should take care of their things.

**Help your children learn about stewardship
in the following ways:**

Sight: As you drive down the street, do some car-watching with your kids. Notice that some old cars are still in very good condition, while some newer cars already look beat up. Talk about what you intend to do to make sure your car doesn't wear down so quickly. Thank God together for providing for your needs.

Sound: Let your kids come up with a list of rules that would help your car stay in top condition. Make sure they explain why that rule will help. (For example: No eating in the car—food stains are hard to clean up.) Ask your kids why they think God wants them to take care of their things.

Touch: Invite your kids to help you work on the car, whether it's changing the tire, cleaning the windows, or overhauling the engine. By getting them involved, you will help them to care more about the day-to-day maintenance of your vehicle. ❁